Doña Gracia Saved Worlds

For Meredith & Frances —B.G.
To all those who love to get lost in beautiful stories. —A.M.

KAR-BEN PUBLISHING®
An imprint of Lerner Publishing Group, Inc.
241 First Avenue North
Minneapolis, MN 55401 USA
Website address: www.karben.com

Main body text set in Charlotte Sans Std. Typeface provided by International Typeface Corp.

Library of Congress Cataloging-in-Publication Data

Names: Goldberg, Bonni, author. | Massari, Alida, illustrator.
Title: Doña Gracia saved worlds / Bonni Goldberg ; illustrated by Alida Massari.
Description: Minneapolis, MN : Kar-Ben Publishing, [2023] | Audience: Ages 5–10 | Audience: Grades 2–3 | Summary: "In 16th
    century Portugal, to be Jewish was to live in secret. Doña Gracia used her wealth and power to escape, helping many other Jews
    to do the same. She built synagogues, hospitals, and schools to help her people"— Provided by publisher.
Identifiers: LCCN 2022040511 (print) | LCCN 2022040512 (ebook) | ISBN 9781728466996 (lib. bdg.) |
    ISBN 9781728495460 (eb pdf)
Subjects: LCSH: Nasi, Gracia, approximately 1510–1569—Juvenile literature. | Jewish women—Portugal—Biography—Juvenile
    literature. | Jews—Portugal—Biography—Juvenile literature. | Crypto-Jews—Portugal—Biography—Juvenile literature. |
    Jews—Europe—Social conditions—16th century. | Portugal—Biography—Juvenile literature.
Classification: LCC DS135.P8 N374 2023 (print) | LCC DS135.P8 (ebook) | DDC 305.892/40469—dc23/eng/20220826

LC record available at https://lccn.loc.gov/2022040511
LC ebook record available at https://lccn.loc.gov/2022040512

Manufactured in the United States of America
1-51638-50389-12/2/2022

Doña Gracia
Saved Worlds

Bonni Goldberg

illustrated by **Alida Massari**

KAR-BEN
PUBLISHING

On Friday nights, Gracia Nasi and her family made sure the doors were locked and the curtains were closed. They whispered their Jewish stories and Sabbath prayers and quietly sang their songs in Ladino, the language of secret Jews.

In sixteenth-century Portugal, all religions except Christianity were against the law.

Even her Jewish name, Gracia, was a secret—*shhh*.

Everyone outside her family called her Beatriz.

But a law couldn't change what Gracia believed in.

At home, in hushed voices, she learned the traditions of her people.

She learned that a person who saves even one life saves a whole world.

Gracia wanted to save worlds.

Gracia grew up and married another secret Jew. Now she was Doña Gracia. Her husband owned the ships that brought spices and silks from the Indies.

Doña Gracia and her husband presented some
of these treasures to the king who agreed,
in return, not to arrest secret Jews.

When Doña Gracia's husband died, he left her in charge of his business.

Many people said that a woman alone wasn't clever enough to run a powerful business.

But still they bought the spicy pepper and the nutty cinnamon her ships brought from faraway lands.

Doña Gracia continued giving gifts to the king to protect her people. She wanted to save worlds.

Practicing Jewish ways in secret became harder and
more dangerous. But no one was allowed to move to
another country.

So Doña Gracia pretended she was making a short trip
to take her nephews to their school in Antwerp. And
she said goodbye to her home in Portugal forever.

But she couldn't leave the other secret Jews behind.
She organized escape plans for them too.

In the darkness of night, secret Jews in Portugal hurried away from their houses. Silently, they climbed aboard the spice ships Doña Gracia had anchored in the harbor.

To keep her Jewish ways, Doña Gracia
had to move to different lands,
seeking safety.

To London.

To Antwerp.

To Venice.

To Ferrara.

Eventually to Istanbul.

London

Antwerp

Lisbon

She wondered if she and her people
would ever be able to stop hiding.

Venice

Ferrara

Istanbul

But wherever she lived, if Doña Gracia heard about secret Jews being captured, she risked arrest to rescue her people. Her messengers faced kidnapping by pirates to free captured Jews.

Doña Gracia was saving worlds.

Finally, the sultan of the great Ottoman Empire invited Doña Gracia to live in Istanbul, where Jews were welcome. No more hiding!

There, every week, Doña Gracia and her family celebrated the Sabbath openly in freedom.

Now that she was safe, Doña Gracia knew it was time to restore the treasures her people had lost in hiding. She helped to print Jewish books and to build synagogues and schools.

Doña Gracia grew old. She dreamed of a land where Jews would be forever free to light their Sabbath candles.

Where the smell of baking challah would fill the air.

Where Jews could gather together to tell their stories, chant their Sabbath prayers, and sing their Ladino songs.

Doña Gracia saved worlds.

Author's Note

Doña Gracia Mendes Nasi (1510–1569)

Doña Gracia lived during a time when, in many countries, Jews, Muslims, and anyone else who wasn't Christian were forced to convert to Christianity. Spain and Portugal had courts called the Inquisition, which searched out and punished converted Christians who still practiced their former religion in secret.

Gracia's Christian name was Beatriz de Luna. Her Jewish name was the ancient Spanish name for Hannah. Gracia married another secret Jew, Francisco Mendes, who, with his brother, Diogo, created a successful trading empire.

Gracia was only twenty-five years old when Francisco's death made her one of the most powerful women of the European Renaissance, in a time when few women had their own wealth or businesses.

When the Inquisition finally came to Portugal, Gracia fled to Antwerp, Belgium, where Diogo lived. They ran the family business together until he died, leaving Gracia in charge of the entire business.

Eventually, Gracia relocated to to Istanbul, then called Constantinople, where she lived openly and safely as a Jew. The Señora Synagogue in Izmir was named after her and still stands today.

It was Doña Gracia's dream to live in the Jewish Holy Land. The Turkish sultan leased the city of Tiberias to her. Doña Gracia died before she could move there. But her nephew, Joseph Nasi, developed one of the first major new Jewish settlements there.